Here Comes The Bride ...And There Goes The Groom

A Comedy in One Act

by Billy St. John

A Samuel French Acting Edition

FOUNDED 1830

SAMUELFRENCH.COM

Copyright © 2002, 2004 by Billy St. John

ALL RIGHTS RESERVED

CAUTION: Professionals and amateurs are hereby warned that HERE COMES THE BRIDE...AND THERE GOES THE GROOM is subject to a royalty. It is fully protected under the copyright laws of the United States of America, the British Commonwealth, including Canada, and all other countries of the Copyright Union. All rights, including professional, amateur, motion picture, recitation, lecturing, public reading, radio broadcasting, television and the rights of translation into foreign languages are strictly reserved. In its present form the play is dedicated to the reading public only.

The amateur live stage performance rights to HERE COMES THE BRIDE... AND THERE GOES THE GROOM are controlled exclusively by Samuel French, Inc., and royalty arrangements and licenses must be secured well in advance of presentation. PLEASE NOTE that amateur royalty fees are set upon application in accordance with your producing circumstances. When applying for a royalty quotation and license please give us the number of performances intended, dates of production, your seating capacity and admission fee. Royalties are payable one week before the opening performance of the play to Samuel French, Inc., at 45 W. 25th Street, New York, NY 10010 or to Samuel French (Canada), Ltd., 100 Lombard Street, Lower Level, Toronto, Ontario, Canada M5C 1M3.

Royalty of the required amount must be paid whether the play is presented for charity or gain and whether or not admission is charged.

Stock royalty quoted upon application to Samuel French, Inc.

For all other rights than those stipulated above, apply to Samuel French, Inc., at 45 West 25th Street, New York, NY 10010.

Particular emphasis is laid on the question of amateur or professional readings, permission and terms for which must be secured in writing from Samuel French, Inc.

Copying from this book in whole or in part is strictly forbidden by law, and the right of performance is not transferable.

Whenever the play is produced the following notice must appear on all programs, printing and advertising for the play: "Produced by special arrangement with Samuel French, Inc."

Due authorship credit must be given on all programs, printing and advertising for the play.

ISBN 978-0-573-60206-1   Printed in U.S.A.   #9988

No one shall commit or authorize any act or omission by which the copyright of, or the right to copyright, this play may be impaired.

No one shall make any changes in this play for the purpose of production.

Publication of this play does not imply availability for performance. Both amateurs and professionals considering a production are strongly advised in their own interests to apply to Samuel French, Inc., for written permission before starting rehearsals, advertising, or booking a theatre.

No part of this book may be reproduced, stored in a retrieval system, or transmitted in any form, by any means, now known or yet to be invented, including mechanical, electronic, photocopying, recording, videotaping, or otherwise, without the prior written permission of the publisher.

IMPORTANT BILLING AND CREDIT REQUIREMENTS

All producers of *HERE COMES THE BRIDE...AND THERE GOES THE GROOM must* give credit to the Author of the Play in all programs distributed in connection with performances of the Play, and in all instances in which the title of the Play appears for the purposes of advertising, publicizing or otherwise exploiting the Play and /or a production. The name of the Author *must* appear on a separate line on which no other name appears, immediately following the title and *must* appear in size of type not less than fifty percent of the size of the title type.

CAST OF CHARACTERS

MILLIE COMPTON — 22, the bride. An attractive young woman. Can be sarcastic when she's upset; at the moment, she's upset.

JULIANNE GORDON — 25, Millie's sister, the matron of honor. Tends to be more level headed and less excitable than Millie.

CAROLYN COMPTON — 50, the mother of the bride, a widow. Is upset, angry, sarcastic, and — at the moment — has a short fuse.

BABS DELANEY — 22, a bridesmaid, Millie's best friend. Outgoing, tries to console Millie.

GEORGIA LAWRENCE — 16, a bridesmaid, the groom's sister. Sweet, somewhat innocent, tries to be a peacemaker.

ALMA ROBERTS — 72, Carolyn's mother, Millie's grandmother. A feisty little old lady, likes to watch male strip shows and mud wrestling.

EMILY LAWRENCE — 46, mother of Georgia and the groom. Extremely upset. Can be very critical.

SYNOPSIS OF SCENES

TIME: The present. A Sunday afternoon.
PLACE: A church dressing room.

(The setting is a dressing room in a church. A door DR opens into the room. A door DL opens out to a bathroom. There is a vanity table with a swivel chair or stool DL. A full length mirror SL faces into the room. A clothes rack is US; on it hangs several garment bags and hangers of clothes. There are a pair of folding chairs SR and three in a line together SL. There are tables and chairs US. The room looks disheveled; there are odd pieces of clothing thrown over some of the tables and chairs US, and shoes, gym bags and purses strew about. The clothing, both hanging and strewn, are the outfits a wedding party has worn to the church before changing into their dressy clothes. AT RISE: The stage is empty. After a beat, the OPENING CHORDS OF THE TRADITIONAL "WEDDING MARCH" IS HEARD BEING PLAYED ON AN ORGAN FAINTLY, as if at a distance, off SR. THE MUSIC PLAYS FOR SEVERAL BEATS, THEN STOPS ABRUPTLY IN THE MIDDLE OF A MEASURE. The stage is still for several beats, then MILLIE COMPTON bursts into the door SR, dressed in a beautiful formal wedding gown and veil. She is followed closely by JULIANNE GORDON, her sister and matron of honor, who wears an appropriate dress or gown. We hear the EXCITED BABBLE OF A CROWD off SR. MILLIE, sobbing, rushes to the vanity DL, tossing her bouquet onto it, flings herself onto the vanity stool, puts her head on the vanity, and cries hysterically. During this, JULIANNE locks the door behind them. She looks at MILLIE a beat, then says:)

JULIANNE. What the hell just happened out there!?!

MILLIE. *(Flinging the veil off her face and over her head to the back.)* You know what happened! You saw it! The love of my life knocked Father Edward into the baptismal font and bolted out the back door!

JULIANNE. I am aware of that. I guess what I'm asking is, why did Pardue leave you standing at the altar?

MILLIE. In the aisle! In the aisle! I didn't even make it to the altar!

JULIANNE. I stand corrected -- in the aisle.

MILLIE. I don't know...

(She breaks into fresh sobs. There is A LOUD POUNDING ON THE DOOR SR.)

CAROLYN. *(Off SR.)* Let me in! Let me in right now!

JULIANNE. It's mother. *(Beat.)* She's upset.

MILLIE. *(Sarcastic.)* How can you tell? She doesn't sound any different than she did when she woke us up in the morning to go to school.

JULIANNE. Should I let her in?

CAROLYN. *(MORE POUNDING; off SR.)* Open this door or I'll rip it off its hinges!!!

JULIANNE. I'd better let her in. *(She unlocks the door and opens it just wide enough for CAROLYN who enters. CAROLYN, MILLIE and JULIANNE'S mother, wears a nice dress or suit with a corsage pinned to her shoulder, a hat, and carries a purse. Whenever the door is opened, we'll hear the BABBLE OF VOICES. To the unseen crowd:)* The rest of you stay out there a minute.

CAROLYN. Millie... *(Crosses hurriedly to MILLIE, stops, then says:)* What the hell just happened out there?

MILLIE. *(Sarcastic.)* Gee, Mother, I don't know. Maybe Pardue suddenly realized the limo was double-parked?

CAROLYN. Is that any way to talk to a woman who's on the verge of hysterics?...and the one who is paying fifty dollars an hour for that limo, by the way.

JULIANNE. Should I send it back to the company? It doesn't look like we'll be needing it.

CAROLYN. *(Impatiently, with a wave of her hand.)* Never mind that now, Julianne. Millie, outside that door are two hundred wedding guests...

JULIANNE. *(Cutting in; to MILLIE.)* Not to mention enough imported paté at the country club to spread over an entire football field. Do you have any idea how many dead French geese gave up the ghost for your benefit?

MILLIE. Why are you two mad at me? I didn't just break the world record for the hundred yard dash -- Pardue did!

JULIANNE. Sorry.

CAROLYN. I'm sorry, too, honey. I'm not angry at you. *(Pacing to SR.)* I only wish I could get my hands around Pardue's neck right now!

MILLIE. Forget it, Mother. You couldn't run fast enough to catch him.

CAROLYN. Not in these shoes, anyway.

(She sits on a chair SR and takes off her shoes.)

JULIANNE. I like those shoes, Mother. Where did you get them?

CAROLYN. *(Squeezing a foot as if it hurts.)* At your friendly, neighborhood S&M store. The only good thing about stopping the wedding is I get to take them off.

MILLIE. I'm glad one of us found something to be thankful for.

JULIANNE. Millie, did you have any idea -- any suspicion -- that your groom was going to take a hike?

MILLIE. No. If I had, I'd have worn a pair of jeans and a sweatshirt with my veil and saved myself the trouble of changing.

CAROLYN. You didn't have a fight? A spat? A difference of opinion?

MILLIE. No, nothing. When could we? After the rehearsal dinner last night, he left for his bachelor party, and I came home with you. I haven't seen him since.

JULIANNE. Unless you count the quick glimpse you got a few minutes ago.

HERE COMES THE BRIDE...AND THERE GOES THE GROOM

MILLIE. That was mostly his back -- it doesn't count.

CAROLYN. *(Taking a lace-trimmed handkerchief from her purse.)* I bought a nice, new handkerchief because I knew I'd be crying before the day was over. *(Beat as she dabs her eyes.)* I should have stuffed a roll of Brawny in this sucker! *(She returns the hanky to her purse.)* I've never been so humiliated in my entire life. Everyone was shocked. I think my uncle Albert had a stroke; with him, it's hard to tell...Your cousin Bonnie fainted. She topped over in the pew like a felled redwood, right onto little Eddie...nearly crushed him. Bonnie really does need to lose weight. She says it's hormonal, but I know better.

MILLIE. Bonnie's size is the least of my worries right now, Mother.

JULIANNE. I bet little Eddie wishes he could say that.

CAROLYN. You're right, Millie. Maybe Pardue said something to his sister. Get Georgia in here.

(JULIANNE unlocks and opens the door a crack. CROWD BABBLE.)

JULIANNE. *(Through the doorway.)* Let Georgia come in -- just Georgia. *(GEORGIA, Pardue's sister, and BABS, Millie's best friend, RUSH IN. They are both nicely dressed in matching bridesmaids' dresses.)* Babs!

BABS. If she's coming in, I am too! *(Rushing DL to MILLIE as JULIANNE closes and locks the door.)* Millie needs her best friend at a time like this! Oh, Millie! Sweetie! *(She leans over MILLIE and hugs her.)* Let me take this off -- that was like hugging a flounder in a fish net. *(She removes MILLIE's veil and tosses it onto the vanity.)* Now... What the hell just happened out there!?!

GEORGIA. You took the words right out of my mouth...well, most of them.

CAROLYN. *(To GEORGIA.)* We were hoping you could tell us.

(BABS sinks onto a chair SL.)

GEORGIA. Me? What makes you think I'd know anything?

CAROLYN. You know what Pardue is like better than the rest of

HERE COMES THE BRIDE...AND THERE GOES THE GROOM 9

us -you've lived under the same roof with your brother for...how old are you?...sixteen years.

GEORGIA. That could be the problem.

CAROLYN. What?

GEORGIA. I mean, Pardue has always lived at home. Mom and Dad could barely afford to send him to college, much less pay for a dorm room. Maybe Pardue realized he'd be moving from our house to his and Millie's apartment without ever having been on his own. Maybe he needs some time to experience independence.

MILLIE. *(Jumping to her feet.)* TODAY he decides he wants to be independent?! We've been engaged for seven months! He had seven months to ask me for his ring back if he was having second thoughts about getting married!

CAROLYN. *(Rising; no nonsense tone of voice.)* You're keeping that ring.

MILLIE. I couldn't wear it now, not after...

CAROLYN. *(Cutting in.)* Who said anything about wearing it? As soon as we get home, I'm going to start looking up pawn shops in the yellow pages.

GEORGIA. Do you have any idea how many nights Pardue flipped hamburgers at McDonald's to pay for that ring?

CAROLYN. No. Do you have any idea how many Big Macs I could get for what this wedding cost me?

(There is a KNOCKING at the door SR.)

ALMA. *(Off SR.)* Carolyn? Millie? Julianne? Are you in there?

JULIANNE. Anyone care to guess what's behind door number one?

MILLIE. Let Grandma Alma in, Julianne.

(JULIANNE unlocks and opens the door a crack. BABBLE NOISES. GEORGIA sinks onto a chair SR. ALMA ENTERS. She is CAROLYN'S mother, MILLIE and JULIANNE'S grandmother. She is nicely dressed, including a hat, wears a corsage and carries a purse. JULIANNE closes the door and locks it.)

ALMA. Millie...Poor thing...If you're through with your veil, can I have it, dear? I'll never be able to show my face in this town again.

MILLIE. You think YOU'll be embarrassed to show your face? I'll have to have plastic surgery!

CAROLYN. As long as you don't expect me to pay for it.

ALMA. Forget I said anything. I guess I'm a little upset.

CAROLYN. Welcome to the club. Sit down, Mama.

(She seats ALMA on a chair SR beside GEORGIA.)

ALMA. That's a pretty dress, Georgia.

GEORGIA. Thank you, Mrs. Roberts.

ALMA. *(Looks over at BABS.)* That's a pretty dress, Babs.

BABS. Thank you, Mrs. Roberts.

MILLIE. *(Getting wound up again.)* What about this dress, Grandma Alma?! It's a knockout, isn't it? Mother paid more for this than she did for the braces on my teeth when I was a kid so I could have a nice smile so I could meet a wonderful man and get married and wear a beautiful dress like this one!...for a grand total of fifteen minutes!

(She runs to the bathroom door SL, crying, and EXITS.)

BABS. *(Rising.)* I'll bathe her face in cold water.

CAROLYN. *(Crossing to BABS, DL.)* Don't get any water on the dress. I plan to dip it in bronze and display it as a lawn ornament. We might as well get some use out of it.

(BABS gives her a wry look, then crosses to the door SL, EXITS, and closes it behind her.)

ALMA. Don't be sarcastic, Carolyn. It isn't becoming.

CAROLYN. I wonder if Father Edward will be conducting any funerals in the next few days? I'd like to crawl in with deceased and just have them put me into the ground.

ALMA. Go back to sarcastic, dear; it beats morbid.

JULIANNE. *(Crossing to CAROLYN.)* Mother, you're worn out.

(She hugs CAROLYN who hugs her back.)

CAROLYN. Last night, after I put on my nightgown, I went to Millie's room, tucked her into bed, like I did when she was a little girl, and sat down beside her. "Millie," I said, "remember, tomorrow, when you're standing at the altar with Pardue by your side, that your dear father is smiling down on you from Heaven above."
JULIANNE. That's sweet, Mother.
CAROLYN. *(Looking Heavenward.)* Jack! If you're up there, can you find Pardue and hurl a lightning bolt at him?
JULIANNE. Mother! You're in a church!
CAROLYN. Do you think he'll do it for me if I light a candle?
JULIANNE. You need to chill out, as the children say. *(She sets CAROLYN on a chair SL.)* I think I have some aspirin in my purse.

(She crosses US; she will find her purse on a table or the rack, open it, take out a bottle of aspirin, and shake out two. Meanwhile:)

CAROLYN. *(Very tired.)* Mama, you didn't warn me there'd be days like this.
ALMA. Carolyn, there'll be days like this.
CAROLYN. Thanks for the advice. Better late than never.
GEORGIA. How depressing. It makes me wonder if I'll ever want to have children.
ALMA. *(Patting her hand.)* Sure you will, Georgia. Sometimes parents have to remind themselves that the good things outweigh the bad. Don't they, Carolyn? *(Long beat; CAROLYN doesn't answer.)* Carolyn?
CAROLYN. Ask me that again, Mama...in about twenty years.
ALMA. *(To GEORGIA.)* Well, they do. Take the advice of an old lady who knows what she's talking about.
CAROLYN. *(She rolls a hand to GEORGIA, the gesture that means "maybe yes, maybe no.")* I have some advice for you, too,

Georgia. If you have a daughter, encourage her to become a nudist; then one day when she announces to you she's engaged, encourage her to get married naked in a meadow with only a bunch of cows as witnesses. You'll thank me for that someday.

(By now JULIANNE has taken the two aspirin and crossed to the door SL.)

JULIANNE. *(Knocking on the door.)* Babs? There are some paper cups by the sink. Will you put some water in one and hand it to me?
BABS. *(Off SL.)* Sure. Hang on a minute. *(MILLIE says something that is muffled off SL.)* Millie said will you get her gym bag? The one with her other clothes in it?
JULIANNE. Okay. *(She crosses to CAROLYN and gives her the aspirin.)* Here, Mother. *(She will look around US and find the right gym bag.)*
CAROLYN. Thank you. I'd rather have Valium. You don't happen to have a couple of Valium you could slip your poor, old mother, do you?
JULIANNE. No. I don't use them.
CAROLYN. Just my luck -- all their lives, I tell my daughters not to do drugs, and now when I need some, I find out they actually listened to me.
ALMA. *(To GEORGIA.)* Carolyn never listened to me when she was little. I told her that wrapping strips of aluminum foil around her wrists would not turn her into Wonder Woman, but she had to try it anyway. She put on her one-piece bathing suit, galoshes, my old rhinestone tiara, a clothesline lasso, and her foil bracelets. Then she told the neighbor's kids to throw rocks at her so she could bounce 'em off her bracelets like bullets.
GEORGIA. What happened?
ALMA. Both arms were in a cast for six weeks.
CAROLYN. Keep it up, Mama. I haven't had enough humiliation heaped on me for one day.
GEORGIA. You mean Wonder Woman was around when you were

HERE COMES THE BRIDE...AND THERE GOES THE GROOM

a child, Mrs. Compton?
CAROLYN. Honey, that broad's old enough to be my mother. *(Cutting her eyes at ALMA.)* I used to wish she WAS my mother.
ALMA. *(Cutting her eyes at CAROLYN.)* So did I.

(After a second, CAROLYN frowns, realizing that ALMA'S comment could be taken two different ways. Her thoughts are interrupted by a KNOCKING ON THE DOOR SR.)

EMILY. *(Off SR.)* Millie? Are you in there? Can I come in? Please?
GEORGIA. Mom... *(Rising; to CAROLYN.)* Can I open the door?
CAROLYN. Why not? Grab one of the other bridesmaids while you're at it, and we can set up a couple of tables for bridge.

(JULIANNE takes MILLIE'S bag to the door SL and raps on it softly. BABS opens the door, takes the bag, and hands out the cup of water and the wedding gown, then closes the door. JULIANNE gives the cup to CAROLYN who downs the aspirin. JULIANNE picks up the bouquet and the veil from the vanity and takes them US. She will put the gown into a garment bag and hang it on the rack. Meanwhile, GEORGIA unlocks the door SR and opens it. There is no babble. EMILY ENTERS. She is PARDUE'S and GEORGIA'S mother. She wears a nice outfit, a hat, and a corsage, and carries a purse.)

EMILY. Georgia... Where's Millie?
GEORGIA. In the bathroom. *(To the others.)* Everyone else has gone.

(She closes the door.)

CAROLYN. Good.
EMILY. Carolyn... *(Rushes to CAROLYN SL and sits SR of her.)* What can I say? I'm so upset...! I'm distraught...! I'm devastated...!
CAROLYN. I can relate to that. Emily, do you know why your son

bolted like a frightened gazelle?

(GEORGIA sits back down beside ALMA.)

    EMILY. No, but I have a suspicion. I'll bet it was that damn bachelor party! Excuse the profanity, Mrs. Roberts.
    ALMA. I've heard worse. *(Beat.)* I've heard worse today.
    CAROLYN. I don't understand. What do you think the bachelor party had to do with it?
    EMILY. Bob, his best man, and the groomsmen took Pardue to Anything Goes last night. It's...*(She glances at ALMA, then lowers her voice.)* It's a strip joint.
    ALMA. I heard that. I've been to a strip joint before -- one that had male strippers.
    CAROLYN. *(A warning.)* Mama...
    ALMA. My friend Florence took me on my seventieth birthday.
    CAROLYN. *(Even more sternly.)* Mama...
    ALMA. I sat on the front row. I had a stiff neck for a week -- you know, from looking up -- but it was worth it.

(GEORGIA is staring at ALMA, fascinated.)

    CAROLYN. Mama! We agreed to keep that little indiscretion in the family!
    ALMA. Emily is almost family...well, she was... Anyway, they announced to everyone that it was my birthday, and El Studdo -- he was the...*(She searches for the right description.)*...biggest attraction -- El Studdo had this candle he wanted me to blow out. You'll never guess where he stuck it!

(JULIANNE wheels around to stare at ALMA.)

    CAROLYN. *(Jumping up.)* Mama!
    GEORGIA. *(Wide eyed.)* Where, Mrs. Roberts?
    EMILY. *(Jumping up.)* Georgia!

ALMA. He...
CAROLYN. MAMA!
EMILY. MRS. ROBERTS!
JULIANNE. GRANDMA ALMA!
ALMA. *(Patting GEORGIA's hand.)* When you're older, dear. *(EMILY and CAROLYN sink back onto their chairs, relieved. Softly, to GEORGIA.)* I'll tell you this much -- I did it with one breath.
CAROLYN. To get back to my previous question, Emily, what do you think the bachelor party had to do with Pardue's sudden case of cold feet?
ALMA. *(Quietly, to GEORGIA.)* My feet stay cold all the time -- poor circulation.
EMILY. Carolyn, I know what strip tease dancers look like -- I've got HBO. They show these documentaries about...well...
GEORGIA. Mom!
EMILY. Your father and I watch them sometimes...on our tv in the bedroom. They can be very educational.
ALMA. Call me the next time one comes on. I have a tv in my bedroom, too.
CAROLYN. Get to the point, Emily.
EMILY. Strippers are usually very attractive...
JULIANNE. Make-up.

(Finished with her chore, she will cross to DL.)

EMILY. ...and they're very well endowed...in the chest area...
JULIANNE. Implants.
EMILY. ...and have long, sexy hair...
JULIANNE. Wigs.

(She sits SL of CAROLYN and EMILY.)

CAROLYN. So?
EMILY. So how can the average young woman compete with them? Watching those strippers, Pardue might have thought, "Do I really want to settle for one cupcake when the bakery is filled with all kinds

of tempting goodies?".

CAROLYN. You're saying Pardue dropped my daughter for a strudel?

JULIANNE. A tart is more like it.

EMILY. It's just a suggestion.

GEORGIA. This isn't like Pardue. He's never even stood up a date before.

JULIANNE. He sure made up for it today. I want to know why he did it. *(To EMILY.)* Mr. Lawrence doesn't know where Pardue went either?

EMILY. No, Julianne, he doesn't. Willard and Bob went to search for him. If he's not at home, Bob knows his usual hangouts.

ALMA. Strip clubs wouldn't be open on a Sunday afternoon.

EMILY. That's not one of his hangouts! He went once!

GEORGIA. Mom... How do you know?

EMILY. Look! I'm sorry I brought it up! I was clutching at straws!

(The door SL opens. BABS and MILLIE ENTER. MILLIE has changed to casual clothes.)

CAROLYN. Do you feel better, Millie?

MILLIE. I feel...numb...

ALMA. *(To GEORGIA.)* My fingers get numb a lot.

EMILY. *(Rises, crosses to MILLIE, and hugs her.)* Millie...sweetheart... What can I say? There is no excuse for Pardue's behavior. I'm so sorry.

MILLIE. Thank you, Mrs. Lawrence. It's not your fault.

EMILY. I'm so glad you feel that way. Nowadays, when something goes wrong, everyone always seems to blame the mother.

CAROLYN. *(Cutting her eyes at ALMA.)* Sometimes there's a good reason for that.

EMILY. If there's anything I can do, don't hesitate to ask.

MILLIE. I won't. Thank you.

(EMILY gives MILLIE another hug, then sits SR of CAROLYN.)

JULIANNE. *(Rising.)* If no one needs the bathroom for a few minutes, I think I'll change clothes too. Grandma Alma?

ALMA. What?

JULIANNE. Do you need to tinkle?

ALMA. No, dear. If I had had to tinkle, I would have tinkled when Father Edward splashed all that water out of the font.

JULIANNE. Just asking. Well, then...

(She crosses US, takes a gym bag or hanger of clothes from the rack and will EXIT SL, closing the door behind her.)

MILLIE. I left my cosmetics out in case I needed to freshen my make-up before we left for the country club. I guess I can put them away now.

BABS. I'll help you.

(They go to the vanity and put the make-up items scattered on it into a cosmetics bag there.)

CAROLYN. *(To MILLIE.)* Since I've already paid Mr. Thomas, I don't suppose you'd consider posing for pictures with one of the groomsmen as a stand-in, would you? Then when you do get married, we can just take some snapshots of the groom and paste his head onto the expensive pictures.

MILLIE. *(An exasperated sigh.)* Mother...

CAROLYN. It was an idea. All the men in a wedding party look pretty much the same except for their heads. A tuxedo is a tuxedo...

MILLIE. At this point, I don't want to ever again think about getting married, but if I do, next time I'll elope.

CAROLYN. *(With great relief.)* Oh, thank you, dear!

EMILY. That sounds very practical. You might consider that too, Georgia.

GEORGIA. Mom! I'm not even going steady!

EMILY. The day will come...

BABS. I love this blush.

MILLIE. Help yourself.
BABS. Thanks.

(She sits at the vanity and applies blush.)

GEORGIA. *(Rising and crossing to DC.)* Millie, what about your honeymoon? Your trip to the Bahamas? Pardue gave me all the tickets to hold for him until you'd changed into your travel clothes and were ready to go.

MILLIE. I don't know...

CAROLYN. Use them. It's too late to get a refund for them, and it'll do you good to get out of town for a few days. Take Babs with you.

BABS. *(Excited.)* To the Bahamas!?! Gee, I'd love to... *(Remembering this is not a joyous occasion, she abruptly switches to a serious tone of voice.)* Millie, if I could be of any comfort to you, I'd certainly be willing to accompany you.

EMILY. *(Frowning.)* Actually, Pardue paid for those tickets... *(CAROLYN gives her a hard stare.)*...but I suppose, under the circumstances, it's only fair that Millie should use them.

MILLIE. I'll think about it.

GEORGIA. I might as well change after Julianne finishes. I'll get my stuff.

(She will cross US and gather clothes, shoes, etc. MILLIE, finished at the vanity except for the blush BABS is using, looks over at ALMA.)

MILLIE. Grandma Alma... *(She crosses to her and will sit beside her.)* This has to be a tiring day for you. How are you holding up?

ALMA. I'm fine, Millie.

MILLIE. You were awfully quiet. What were you thinking about?

ALMA. I wish I had got to show off my pretty new dress more. I was trying to remember if there are any funerals this afternoon for anybody I know.

CAROLYN. Keep it on. When I get a hold of Pardue, there might be. *(Realizing.)* Emily, I'm sorry. I shouldn't have said that.

EMILY. That's all right, Carolyn. I know you didn't mean it.

CAROLYN. Oh, I meant it...I just didn't mean to say it in front of a witness who'd tell.

MILLIE. *(A warning.)* Mother...

EMILY. *(Irritated.)* I realize that comment was a feeble attempt at a joke, Carolyn, but it was made in very poor taste...like quite a lot of the things I've heard you say the few times we've been together.

GEORGIA. *(A warning.)* Mom...

CAROLYN. *(Rising.)* If you're implying you think I'm crude, just come right out and say it, Emily.

EMILY. *(Rising.)* All right. I think you're an extremely sarcastic woman.

ALMA. Don't blame me -- I tried.

EMILY. What's more, I've heard some pretty stinging remarks come out of Millie's mouth sometimes, as well...a trait she picked up from you, no doubt.

MILLIE. *(Rising; surprised.)* Mrs. Lawrence!

BABS. Uh...ladies...This has been a very tense day for all of us, and...

CAROLYN. *(Cutting in.)* Babs, after all the years you've been friends with Millie I've come to think of you as another daughter, so I can say this to you without hesitation: mind your own business!

EMILY. Babs, I don't know you from Adam's house cat: butt out!

MILLIE. *(Crossing to EMILY; frostily.)* Mrs. Lawrence, I would appreciate it if you wouldn't talk to my friend like that. There -- was that civil enough for you?

BABS. It's all right...really...

GEORGIA. All of you, please...don't do this.

ALMA. Let 'em get it out of their systems, girls. I haven't seen a good fight since Florence took me to mud wrestling.

EMILY. Don't be ridiculous! We're not going to fight!

CAROLYN. Chicken, huh?

EMILY. Why, you...!

(She swings her purse and hits CAROLYN on the upper arm. CAROLYN hits EMILY's arm with her purse. The fight is on! It consists of them

smacking each other's arms with their purses and kicking at each other's legs. MILLIE grabs EMILY around the waist from behind as BABS jumps up and grabs CAROLYN the same way. They attempt to pull them apart. Everyone in the scene ad-libs excitedly.)

CAROLYN. *(After getting kicked in the leg.)* Ow! No fair! You still have your shoes on!
EMILY. Some of us around here don't behave like hillbillies!

(More fur flies.)

ALMA. *(Jumping up.)* Whoopie! *(Bouncing up and down with excitement.)* Knock the stuffings out of her!
GEORGIA. Mrs. Roberts! Don't tell her to hit my mother!
ALMA. I was talking TO your mother! Maybe SHE can teach Carolyn to watch her mouth. *(To EMILY.)* You go, girl!

(Hearing the commotion, JULIANNE RUNS IN SL. She has changed to casual clothes.)

JULIANNE. What in the world...? *(She hurries to between EMILY and CAROLYN, separating them.)* Mrs. Lawrence! Mother! Stop it right now! *(CAROLYN and EMILY stop swatting at each other.)* You should be ashamed of yourselves! Both of you!
ALMA. That was fun while it lasted.

(She sits back down.)

JULIANNE. Mrs. Lawrence, come over here.

(She leads her SR and seats her beside ALMA.)

MILLIE. Really, Mother! You could have hurt each other!
CAROLYN. I tried; I'd have licked her if I had remembered to take my Centrum Silver this morning.

MILLIE. What am I going to do with you?

BABS. You could sign her up for karate lessons. I think she has a lot of potential.

MILLIE. Babs -- zip it up!

JULIANNE. *(To EMILY.)* Try to relax.

MILLIE. You, too, Mother.

(She and BABS sit on the chairs SL, pulling CAROLYN down between them)

ALMA. *(To EMILY.)* Those were some kicks you got in.

EMILY. Thank you. I work out with my Thigh Master.

ALMA. Does he make house calls?

JULIANNE. Hush, Grandma Alma. *(To everyone.)* Now...What was that all about?

GEORGIA. My mother got angry at something your mother said about my brother.

CAROLYN. Why don't we round up all of our aunts and uncles and cousins and make it a real family feud? *(To MILLIE.)* We could roll Bonnie at them and knock over her whole clan like bowling pins.

JULIANNE. There's not going to be any more feuding!

CAROLYN. If you say so, but would you bring me my shoes? I want to be ready next time, just in case...

(JULIANNE picks up Carolyn's shoes where she left them by the chairs SR and takes them to her. CAROLYN will put them on. JULIANNE will sit on the vanity stool.)

ALMA. *(Quietly, to EMILY.)* Don't turn your back on her -- she can be real sneaky.

GEORGIA. *(Crossing to DC.)* So, what's your punishment going to be, Mom?

EMILY. What?

GEORGIA. When I got into a fight in the fourth grade, you made me go for a week without watching tv. It's only right that you should be punished, too.

EMILY. *(Exasperated.)* Oh, Georgia...

CAROLYN. That was when there were some good programs on tv. Considering the junk they show now, you should make her WATCH television for a week.

GEORGIA. Good suggestion. If things have settled down, I'll go change.

JULIANNE. *(Rising.)* Let me get my dress out of the way.

(GEORGIA will take her clothes and EXIT SL. JULIANNE will go into the bathroom with her, then come back out with her dress, close the door, cross US, put her dress into a garment bag, and hang it on the rack.)

EMILY. *(To CAROLYN.)* I'll thank you not to give my daughter advice, Carolyn. If she needs any, I'll give it to her.

CAROLYN. It doesn't concern me what advice you might give Georgia, but I wish you had given some to Pardue. Didn't you ever point out to him that it's rude to leave a bride waiting at the altar?

MILLIE & JULIANNE. *(Together.)* In the aisle.

CAROLYN. Whatever.

EMILY. That is not something a mother...or father...usually thinks it's necessary to tell a son, Carolyn. If you had had any boys, you'd realize that.

CAROLYN. I'll take your word for it. Maybe somebody should write and suggest they include that tip the next time they update Emily Post.

MILLIE. That's a good idea, Mother. I'll E-mail the publisher as soon as we get home. Old Emily...*(To EMILY.)* Post, not you...omitted quite a few rules of etiquette she should have included.

ALMA. Like don't pass gas. In church. That's not in the book, either. I checked.

EMILY. Is this what it's always like at your house? Three generations of you sitting around cracking jokes all the time?

BABS. I can answer that, Mrs. Lawrence. Yes, it is. I love to go to

HERE COMES THE BRIDE...AND THERE GOES THE GROOM

Millie's -- it's more entertaining than any tv sitcom I've ever seen.

JULIANNE. We're a family that enjoys life, Mrs. Lawrence. If you can joke about even the bad things that happen, it's better than crying.

EMILY. Like now?

MILLIE. Exactly...but this one is a little harder to get through than most.

ALMA. This is worse than the time I set the dog on fire...but that's another story. *(To EMILY.)* It was an accident. Killer is fine now.

EMILY. What kind of dog is he?

ALMA. A hairless chihuahua.

EMILY. Why does that not surprise me? *(Turning to CAROLYN.)* Carolyn, even though I didn't like what you said about Pardue, I'm sorry I lost my temper.

CAROLYN. Me, too.

(There is a long beat of silence. CAROLYN cuts her eyes toward EMILY to see if it registered that "Me, too" wasn't necessarily an apology. There is the MUFFLED SOUND OF A CELL PHONE RINGING. MILLIE and BABS rise and cross US where they and JULIANNE find their purses and look in them for their phones. As they do this, ALMA, EMILY and CAROLYN search their purses which they have with them.)

GEORGIA. *(Off SL.)* Mom, if that's my phone, will you get it?

(Everyone brings out a phone.)

EMILY. It's mine. *(The others put their phones back into their purses as EMILY punches a button on hers and puts it to her ear.)* Hello?...oh...well...see what Bob can come up with...bye, Willard. *(She pushes a button and puts the phone back into her purse. To all:)* Pardue isn't at our house.

MILLIE. Don't keep searching for him on my account. At this point, I never want to see him or talk to him again.

JULIANNE. I do. He owes us an explanation.

CAROLYN. A good one...if there is any such thing. I keep hoping I'll wake up to discover this has all been a really bad dream.

ALMA. I had a bad dream recently. I drempt that I was walking through a crowded department store in nothing but my underwear.

CAROLYN. That wasn't a dream, Mama. You were trying on clothes at J. C. Penney's and forgot to put your dress back on.

ALMA. I guess that's why they won't let me shop there anymore.

(GEORGIA ENTERS SL, carrying her dress. She has changed to casual clothes.)

GEORGIA. Who was it?
EMILY. Your father. Pardue isn't home.
GEORGIA. Oh. *(Indicating the bathroom.)* Next?
BABS. I guess that would be me.

(She will get her clothes and EXIT SL, closing the door. GEORGIA will put her dress into a garment bag and hang it on the rack.)

GEORGIA. What do we do now?
MILLIE. I suppose we should clean up the dressing room and go.
GEORGIA. Go where?
EMILY. I told some of our relatives and friends to drive over to the country club and wait for us there. I said we'd join them and explain everything later.

(MILLIE, GEORGIA and JULIANNE begin to clean up the mess US.)

CAROLYN What are you going to tell them?
EMILY. I don't know. If I'm lucky, a giant pothole will open up in the road and swallow my car before I get there.

ALMA. I hope someone saves me a piece of cake.

CAROLYN. Nobody's going to cut the cake, Mama. The bride and groom always cut the cake. I have an idea we'll all be eating hunks of frozen wedding cake for years.

JULIANNE. Should I call the caterers and have them set out the

shrimp and paté?
CAROLYN. You might as well.

(In the background, JULIANNE will take her phone from her purse, call a number, and ad-lib a quiet conversation with the caterers.)

ALMA. Paté? Is that that stuff that looks like Alpo on a cracker? Peu! That mess makes me gag! Feed it to the dogs!
CAROLYN. Paté is goose liver, Mama.
ALMA. I got goosed last Friday...at the senior citizens' center. By Leroy Spitzer. Leroy's got the hots for me. He thinks I'm a foxy mama. He's been trying to get me to come over to his apartment. He said he'd give me a rubdown.
GEORGIA. With exotic oils and lotions, Mrs. Roberts?
EMILY. Georgia!
ALMA. With Ben-Gay. I might take him up on it.
CAROLYN. You most certainly will not!
ALMA. Spoilsport. If you had your way, I'd never have any fun.
CAROLYN. If I had my way, you'd be locked up in a detention home for incorrigible old ladies!

(BABS ENTERS SL, carrying her dress. She has changed to casual clothes. JULIANNE finishes her phone conversation, rings off, and puts her phone back into her purse.)

BABS. What are we doing?
MILLIE. Packing up to go home.

(BABS will put her dress into a garment bag and hang it on the rack.)

EMILY. *(Rising.)* I'm not getting anything accomplished sitting here. I'll see if there are any guests still hanging around and send them away.
CAROLYN. Send them to the club with the others. I've got tons of food to get rid of...if anyone has an appetite.

ALMA. I do.
CAROLYN. Fine, Mama. I ordered five hundred cheese puffs for the reception. They're yours.
ALMA. Oh, goodie.

(There is the MUFFLED RINGING OF A CELL PHONE. Again, everyone stops what they're doing and digs in their purses for their phones.)

MILLIE. It's mine, this time. *(Punches a button.)* Hello?...Pardue!

(Everyone else turns to watch her, anxiously.)

ALMA. Who is it?
CAROLYN. Benedict Arnold.
ALMA. *(To EMILY.)* That must be one of your guests.
MILLIE. Yes...yes... *(She will cross slowly to DL and sit on the vanity stool.)* Oh, no...really?...oh, Pardue...
EMILY. Is he all right?

(MILLIE nods "yes" to her.)

CAROLYN. For now, maybe...
MILLIE. Where are you?...uh-huh...I understand...I understand completely...yes...as soon as I can...goodbye, darling.

(She rings off, smiling.)

CAROLYN. Darling? *(Looking Heavenward.)* Jack? Hold that lightning bolt!
BABS. Where is he, Millie!?! What happened!?! Don't keep us in suspense!
ALMA. Did he run off with a stripper?
JULIANNE. Hush, Grandma Alma. Millie...?
MILLIE. *(Turning to them, beaming.)* He's in the men's restroom –

— here in the church.
GEORGIA. The restroom?
MILLIE. He said when he saw me coming down the aisle, he got so nervous he had this sudden urge to throw up. He said he didn't have time to explain -- that he had to get to a restroom right away. He barely made it.
GEORGIA. He's been throwing up all this time?
MILLIE. He said he thinks he even tossed up a tuna fish sandwich he ate last Wednesday. As soon as he was sure he was through, he washed his face and called me. *(Rising.)* He still wants to get married!
CAROLYN. *(A hand on her chest.)* I think my heart started beating again. It must have stopped thirty minutes ago.
ALMA. It's hard to tell sometimes.
EMILY. I should have guessed. When Pardue was six years old, he played the turkey in his first grade Thanksgiving pageant. The school auditorium was packed with parents and relatives and friends. Just before the show was to start, Pardue peeped out at the audience. I saw his little turkey head sticking out at the edge of the curtain for a second, then pop back out of sight. A few minutes later, Mrs. Holloway, his teacher, came out. She told us the start of the program would be delayed due to a minor problem backstage. Sure enough, about fifteen minutes later the pageant went on. Mrs. Holloway told me later that when he saw the audience, Pardue had the worse case of stage fright she had ever seen. He threw up then, too -- all over a little girl who was playing a pumpkin. The show couldn't go on till Mrs. Holloway had cleaned them both up. But it did go on. Pardue was wonderful, if I do say so myself.
CAROLYN. *(Sarcastic.)* I must have missed the review in the New York Times.

(EMILY shoots her a look.)

BABS. So you're saying Pardue left Millie standing at the altar...
MILLIE & JULIANNE. *(Together: cutting in.)* In the aisle.
BABS. ...in the aisle because he had stage fright?
EMILY. Evidently.

GEORGIA. What do you know about that?
ALMA. Only what she told us.
MILLIE. Pardue is just as brave now as he was when he was six years old. In spite of how nervous he feels, he wants to go on with the ceremony. We're getting married!

(GEORGIA and BABS cheer.)

CAROLYN. Now? Oh my god, you've got to change clothes!
JULIANNE. *(Meaning her, BABS and GEORGIA.)* So do we!

(The place turns into Bedlam. MILLIE rushes US where she, BABS, GEORGIA and JULIANNE tear frantically through the clothes as they search for their dresses.)

CAROLYN. *(Rises; taking charge.)* Julianne, wait! Call the caterers! Tell them the reception has been delayed, but that it will go on! Have them send everyone who's already arrived back to the church!
JULIANNE. Yes, Mother.

(She grabs her purse, gets her phone and makes the call.)

ALMA. There go my cheese puffs.
CAROLYN. Emily! Call your husband and tell him to have Pardue's best man here in record time! *(EMILY starts digging in her purse for her phone. She will ad-lib the call to Willard.)* I'll hit the parking lot and herd anyone I find back inside! We need to find Father Edward! Do any of you have any idea where he could be?
EMILY. *(Covering the phone with her hand.)* There's a laundry room with a washer and dryer in the church basement! He might be drying his clothes!
CAROLYN. Good thinking! *(A quick smile passes between CAROLYN and EMILY. Things are okay between them again.)* Mama! Will you see if you can find Father Edward in the laundry room?
ALMA. I'll be glad to. Do you suppose he'll be naked?

CAROLYN. Knock first! Now, hurry!

ALMA. I will, but there's something I need to do first. *(At this point, MILLIE, carrying her wedding dress, opens the bathroom door and is about to exit.)* Millie! *(MILLIE stops and turns to ALMA.)* Wait a minute, dear.

The others stop to watch ALMA as she crosses to MILLIE, thinking they're about to hear some tender words of advice from grandmother to granddaughter.)

MILLIE. *(To ALMA, gently, when she reaches her.)* Yes, Grandma Alma? What did you wish to tell me?

ALMA. NOW I need to tinkle!

ALMA EXITS SL, closing the door. MILLIE stands beside it, smiling, as the others resume their frantic activity. The hubbub continues as the lights fade to BLACKOUT.)

CURTAIN

PROPS

PRE-SET:

Cosmetics including blush, Cosmetics bag -- on vanity
Clothing, garment bags, gym bags -- scattered US
7 cell phones -- 1 in each actress' purse

PERSONAL:

Bouquet -- Millie
Diamond ring -- Millie
Purse w/handkerchief -- Carolyn
Purse w/aspirin bottle/2 aspirin -- Julianne
Paper cup w/water -- Babs
Purse -- Alma

COSTUME PLOT

MILLIE -- wedding gown, veil, shoes, casual outfit

JULIANNE -- matron of honor dress, shoes, casual outfit

CAROLYN -- mother of the bride dress or suit, hat, shoes, purse, corsage

BABS -- bridesmaid dress, shoes, casual outfit

GEORGIA -- bridesmaid dress, shoes, casual outfit

ALMA -- grandmother of the bride dress or suit, hat, shoes, purse, corsage

EMILY -- mother of the groom dress or suit, hat, shoes, purse, corsage

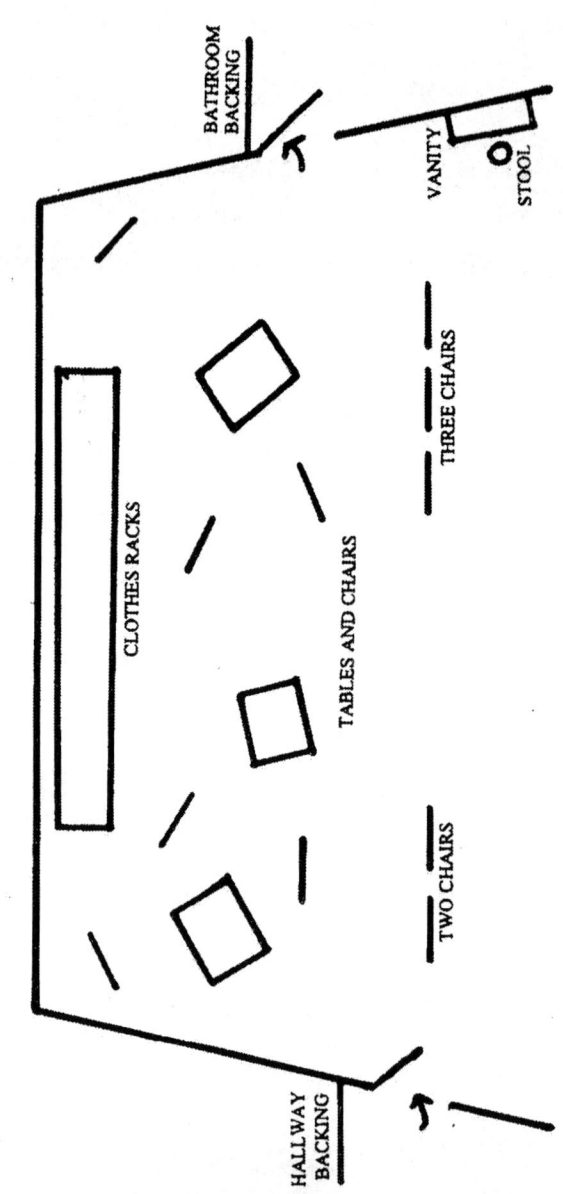

"HERE COMES THE BRIDE...AND THERE GOES THE GROOM"

OTHER TITLES AVAILABLE FROM SAMUEL FRENCH

CAPTIVE
Jan Buttram

Comedy / 2m, 1f / Interior

A hilarious take on a father/daughter relationship, this off beat comedy combines foreign intrigue with down home philosophy. Sally Pound flees a bad marriage in New York and arrives at her parent's home in Texas hoping to borrow money from her brother to pay a debt to gangsters incurred by her husband. Her elderly parents are supposed to be vacationing in Israel, but she is greeted with a shotgun aimed by her irascible father who has been left home because of a minor car accident and is not at all happy to see her. When a news report indicates that Sally's mother may have been taken captive in the Middle East, Sally's hard-nosed brother insists that she keep father home until they receive definite word, and only then will he loan Sally the money. Sally fails to keep father in the dark, and he plans a rescue while she finds she is increasingly unable to skirt the painful truths of her life. The ornery father and his loveable but slightly-dysfunctional daughter come to a meeting of hearts and minds and solve both their problems.

SAMUELFRENCH.COM

OTHER TITLES AVAILABLE FROM SAMUEL FRENCH

TAKE HER, SHE'S MINE
Phoebe and Henry Ephron

Comedy / 11m, 6f / Various Sets

Art Carney and Phyllis Thaxter played the Broadway roles of parents of two typical American girls enroute to college. The story is based on the wild and wooly experiences the authors had with their daughters, Nora Ephron and Delia Ephron, themselves now well known writers. The phases of a girl's life are cause for enjoyment except to fearful fathers. Through the first two years, the authors tell us, college girls are frightfully sophisticated about all departments of human life. Then they pass into the "liberal" period of causes and humanitarianism, and some into the intellectual lethargy of beatniksville. Finally, they start to think seriously of their lives as grown ups. It's an experience in growing up, as much for the parents as for the girls.

"A warming comedy. A delightful play about parents vs kids. It's loaded with laughs. It's going to be a smash hit."
– *New York Mirror*

SAMUELFRENCH.COM

SAMUEL FRENCH STAFF

Nate Collins
President

Ken Dingledine
Director of Operations,
Vice President

Bruce Lazarus
Executive Director,
General Counsel

Rita Maté
Director of Finance

ACCOUNTING
Lori Thimsen | Director of Licensing Compliance
Nehal Kumar | Senior Accounting Associate
Glenn Halcomb | Royalty Administration
Jessica Zheng | Accounts Receivable
Andy Lian | Accounts Payable
Charlie Sou | Accounting Associate
Joann Mannello | Orders Administrator

BUSINESS AFFAIRS
Caitlin Bartow | Assistant to the Executive Director

CORPORATE COMMUNICATIONS
Abbie Van Nostrand | Director of Corporate Communications

CUSTOMER SERVICE AND LICENSING
Brad Lohrenz | Director of Licensing Development
Laura Lindson | Licensing Services Manager
Kim Rogers | Theatrical Specialist
Matthew Akers | Theatrical Specialist
Ashley Byrne | Theatrical Specialist
Jennifer Carter | Theatrical Specialist
Annette Storckman | Theatrical Specialist
Dyan Flores | Theatrical Specialist
Sarah Weber | Theatrical Specialist
Nicholas Dawson | Theatrical Specialist
David Kimple | Theatrical Specialist

EDITORIAL
Amy Rose Marsh | Literary Manager
Ben Coleman | Literary Associate

MARKETING
Ryan Pointer | Marketing Manager
Courtney Kochuba | Marketing Associate
Chris Kam | Marketing Associate

PUBLICATIONS AND PRODUCT DEVELOPMENT
Joe Ferreira | Product Development Manager
David Geer | Publications Manager
Charlyn Brea | Publications Associate
Tyler Mullen | Publications Associate
Derek P. Hassler | Musical Products Coordinator
Zachary Orts | Musical Materials Coordinator

OPERATIONS
Casey McLain | Operations Supervisor
Elizabeth Minski | Office Coordinator, Reception
Coryn Carson | Office Coordinator, Reception

SAMUEL FRENCH BOOKSHOP (LOS ANGELES)
Joyce Mehess | Bookstore Manager
Cory DeLair | Bookstore Buyer
Sonya Wallace | Bookstore Associate
Tim Coultas | Bookstore Associate
Alfred Contreras | Shipping & Receiving

LONDON OFFICE
Anne-Marie Ashman | Accounts Assistant
Felicity Barks | Rights & Contracts Associate
Steve Blacker | Bookshop Associate
David Bray | Customer Services Associate
Robert Cooke | Assistant Buyer
Stephanie Dawson | Amateur Licensing Associate
Simon Ellison | Retail Sales Manager
Robert Hamilton | Amateur Licensing Associate
Peter Langdon | Marketing Manager
Louise Mappley | Amateur Licensing Associate
James Nicolau | Despatch Associate
Martin Phillips | Librarian
Panos Panayi | Company Accountant
Zubayed Rahman | Despatch Associate
Steve Sanderson | Royalty Administration Supervisor
Douglas Schatz | Acting Executive Director
Roger Sheppard | I.T. Manager
Debbie Simmons | Licensing Sales Team Leader
Peter Smith | Amateur Licensing Associate
Garry Spratley | Customer Service Manager
David Webster | UK Operations Director
Sarah Wolf | Rights Director

SAMUELFRENCH.COM
SAMUELFRENCH-LONDON.CO.UK

Get the name of your cast and crew in print with Special Editions!

Special Editions are a unique, fun way to commemorate your production and RAISE MONEY.

The Samuel French Special Edition is a customized script personalized to *your* production. Your cast and crew list, photos from your production and special thanks will all appear in a Samuel French Acting Edition alongside the original text of the play.

These Special Editions are powerful fundraising tools that can be sold in your lobby or throughout your community in advance.

These books have autograph pages that make them perfect for year book memories, or gifts for relatives unable to attend the show. Family and friends will cherish this one of a kind souvenier.

Everyone will want a copy of these beautiful, personalized scripts!

Order Your copies today!
E-mail SpecialEditions@samuelfrench.com
or call us at 1-866-598-8449!